Praise for Birdseed

"Catrina Lee [Anam Cara Cat] helps students bridge the gap between happiness and academic success by making both the practice of joy and the practice of writing a daily activity."
—Shawn Achor, NY Times Bestselling Author of Before Happiness

"There are so many books that try to motivate and guide adults. Yet there are few that focus on children, a population in desperate need of such inspiration. In addition, it is rare to find self-improvement or motivation taught in the classroom. I commend Catrina Lee [Anam Cara Cat] for writing *Birdseed* and bringing children this wonderful gift of self-love."
—Dr. Charles F. Glassman, MD FACP, "Coach MD," Practitioner of Internal Medicine with Emphasis in Prevention & Wellness, New York, USA

"Mindfulness and Social-Emotional Learning have become areas of increased interest and growth within the field of education. However, incorporating the practices associated with these focus areas into a classroom environment is the challenge facing educators. In her book, *Birdseed*, Catrina Lee [Anam Cara Cat] provides a powerful, yet simple example of how to integrate these activities into a classroom environment. She makes the practice approachable, usable and do-able! This book will serve as the catalyst for connecting to and with your students for years to come!"
—Jessica Daily, MTSS Systems Support Coordinator, Colorado Department of Education, CO, USA

"Extremely refreshing and encouraging that someone finally speaks of the idea of nurturing the curiosity and zest of these young souls. From Aristotle to Zig Ziglar this book provides a spectrum of thought, reflection and mindfulness."
—Mark Young, Psy. D., Doctor of Psychology & Facilitator for At-Risk Youth, CO, USA

"Birdseed is long overdue in classrooms everywhere. It is a program that encourages intellectual development through our creative humanity. The daily exercises stimulate the growth of new networks in young promising brains, while simultaneously leading our kids toward lives of meaning and integrity. Bravo to innovators like Catrina Lee [Anam Cara Cat]."
—*Joan Block M.A, Marriage and Family Therapist, CO, USA*

"There are gift-givers in the world who intuit the right action at the right time with right intention, and with great love, act with purpose to the benefit of humanity. In *Birdseed*, Anam Cara Cat gifts us all with the reminder that young souls are hungry and must be fed. It is no small thing to nourish a generation of youth, and this one starves for meaning. We cannot forget the whole child in the frenzy of academic achievement. This offering of a classroom protocol is both educationally valid and good, solid nourishment. Bravo!"
—*Lisa Burns PhD, Teacher, Psychotherapist, & Cofounder of Sozo Youth Sanctuary Foundation, CO, USA*

"The value of developing children's socio-emotional capacities and offering them opportunities to explore the meaning of being open minded citizens of the world cannot be underestimated. This book challenges us as teachers to look into our own characters as well as facilitating character building in children."
—*Natalia Gardener, Sports Education, University of Wolverhampton, UK*

"As a passionate, and somewhat stereotypical, mathematics teacher, I have never worried about my students failing their exams, but I confess, I often worry about them failing in life. Now, with the magic of *Birdseed* on my side, this worry diminishes."
—*Elizabeth Orchard, Master of Science, Rugby, England*

"A treasury of quotes and ideas."
—Roger Smith, Teacher, Association for Support of International Education, Biot, France

"As a senior leader in a school in Greater London catering for pupils with autism, I actively promote what Anam Cara Cat so beautifully embodies via this beautiful resource. I cannot recommend this book enough."
—Jules Ruddick, Assistant Head Teacher, Middlesex, England

"*Birdseed* is the perfect tool for provoking inspiring thought in students. It provides such a beautiful outlet to get students thinking beyond the walls of the classroom and into their infinite selves. Give your students "Birdseed" and you give them wings to fly!"
—Ayeshah Tahirah, K-12 Teacher, Vienna, Austria

"Birdseeds were always something I looked forward to throughout my week. They continuously inspired me to be better, do better, and to aspire to achieve my goals. These inspirational quotes provided me with a positive outlook on life and really did have such a great impact on my day to day learning."
—Selin Hassan, London, UK, Former Student

"I loved starting the day with Birdseed! Such fantastic positive energy to get you started on the day and keeps you inspired! The daily practice made me feel like a better person and taught me to be a more kind-hearted person towards everyone around me!
—Erden Karso, Hendrik-Ido-Ambacht, Netherlands, Former Student

"Starting the day with a Birdseed was like morning breakfast nutrition that gave me wisdom to chew on throughout the day. It made me see certain aspects of life in a different way and helped me to tackle situations with a different perspective. I looked forward to it every day.

—Selin Gecit, Istanbul, Turkey, Former Student

"Birdseed simply sets the day off right, as it's not only a warm-up exercise, but additionally allows one to reflect and grow positively as a person. In my case especially, it gave me a more positive and grateful outlook on my day-to-day life, showing how precious each day in reality is."

—Zuzia Dzieciol, Czerwonak Poland, Former Student

"I remember a day when everyone in our class was very depressed after doing a difficult exam, and everyone feared they would fail. When we went to English class right after, with everyone feeling horrible, Ms. Lee shared a Birdseed that inspired us to overcome the fear of failure and accept our mistakes."

—Jasmine Shahbazi, Dubai , United Arab Emirates, Former Student

"The Birdseed quotes were truly inspirational; they always left me feeling optimistic and passionate. It taught me how to be more open-minded and look at my surroundings from a different perspective. Something I will appreciate for years to come."

—Perla Gabay, Stockholm Sweden, Former Student

Birdseed

A Guide to Teaching Emotional Intelligence

in the Primary & Secondary Classroom

Daily Activity to Foster

Social-Emotional Development & Personal Growth

By Anam Cara Cat

<u>Sample Quotes:</u>

"Everybody is a genius, but if you judge a fish by its ability to climb a tree, it will go its whole life believing that it is stupid." ~ *Albert Einstein*

"Never doubt that a single person can change the world. Indeed it's the only thing that ever has."
~ *Margaret Mead*

"Man cannot discover new oceans unless he has the courage to lose sight of the shore." ~ *Andre Gide*

"The greater danger for most of us lies not in setting our aim too high and falling short, but in setting our aim too low, and achieving our mark." ~ *Michelangelo*

"Keep away from people who try to belittle your ambitions. Small people always do that, but the really great make you feel that you, too, can become great." ~ *Mark Twain*

"Don't ask what the world needs. Ask what makes you come alive and go do it because what the world needs is more people who have come alive."
~ *Howard Thurman*

"Great spirits have always encountered violent opposition from mediocre minds." ~ *Albert Einstein*

For Jack, who embodied the soul of teaching and

believed in the Higher Calling...

And for my students, who wholeheartedly taught me

about life, love, and learning

Contents

"We must believe in the power and strength of our words.

Our words can change the world."

~ Malala Yousafzai

Preface

After teaching high school for more than a decade, I have learned the immeasurable value of teaching Emotional Intelligence in the classroom. Since learning the elusive art and science behind happiness, I recognize that teaching students to manage their emotions is the foundation of social-emotional learning. Until they develop primary intrapersonal competencies, they simply lack the capacity to increase self-awareness or strengthen the other facets of the social-emotional domain such as interpersonal skills, empathy, curiosity, self-motivation, and resilience. Simply put, the better students feel, the more receptive they are as learners.

Ultimately, we want for our students, and every child, the same thing we all want for ourselves: happiness. Because we believe success *leads* to happiness, we fervently focus on guiding students to define and refine their visions of success; then, we direct them to create specific goals and to concentrate their efforts and attention on the concrete steps to achievement. Happiness is, either explicitly or implicitly, presented as the reward for hard work and dedication. However, research has proven something is painfully amiss with this approach. If we take a wide look around, even at those considered "successful," few people are genuinely and habitually happy. Sadly, a large majority of people have either given up on happiness altogether or they're in an endless *pursuit* of it. The seemingly mythic experience of ever-lasting joy more closely resembles an epic fairy tale than everyday reality, which begs the question: Why?

Neuroscientists and psychologists have sought to answer that question for eons. Fortunately, progressive efforts have led to promising findings that confirm happiness is available to everyone, regardless of one's circumstances or station in life. This is because happiness is both a skill and a habit that can be *learned*, not an inherent quality that is fortuitously embodied by the few. Furthermore, research reflects that happy people are irrefutably more successful *because* they are happy, not the other way around. This may seem counterintuitive since the traditional formula for happiness ingrained in Western society is:

hard work = success = happiness.

But herein lies the problem. This formula is backwards. Studies show that pleasure experienced as the result of achieving goals and attaining success is sorely short-lived. This is because as soon as one's vision of success (whatever that looks like) is realized, the sense of satisfaction and fulfillment soon wears off and another vision takes its place. Once you reach one milestone, you set your sights on the next milestone; once you attain one level of accomplishment, you aspire for a higher level of accomplishment; once you acquire the material things you want, you tire of them and want new things... and so-on and so-forth.

This pattern is especially prevalent in adolescence and often plays out in the erroneous belief that an external thing or person will bring happiness. Deceptive thoughts pervade students' daily existence such as: if I get these grades, if I drive this car, if I date this person, if I get this job, if I wear these clothes, if I look like that, if I lose this weight...then I will be happy. They don't realize—and won't realize—until they attain those aims that such notions of happiness are illusory and leave them still wanting for more.

Whether our students are focused on achieving academic objectives, occupational goals, social standards, or all of the above, if happiness is dependent solely on arriving at some set point in the future, it will always be just beyond reach. Happiness will be a *pursuit* of something that will exist "someday" instead of an *experience* that exists in the Now. Rather than hope they eventually learn this through trial and error, why not expose them to a paradigm that better serves them and orients them for success AND happiness?

Positive psychology guru and Harvard graduate Shawn Achor is one of the world's leading experts on the connection between happiness and success. He has devoted decades of his life to studying the proverbial treadmill and teaching others how to recognize and rectify the fallacies we've all been fed related to joy and fulfillment. His work has had a profound effect on my own perspective in life and has had a major influence on how I now approach the topics of success and happiness with my high school students.

Achor's bestselling books *The Happiness Advantage* and *Before Happiness* explore the misconceptions of achieving and sustaining happiness and emphasize the importance of reversing our formula for success. He recognizes a problem that plagues much of society: the idea that happiness is always just around the corner, tied to some measure of achievement; then he offers a solution: teach happiness as a skill, stressing that it's the *precursor* to success, not the result of it.

Achor asserts that the greatest predictor of one's success has less to do with hard skills and external factors and everything to do with how he or she feels and perceives the world. Therefore, the best way educators can serve future generations is to acknowledge emotional intelligence—particularly happiness—as a critical building block for lifelong learning and achievement and address it accordingly. It is crucial that we teach students how to retrain their brains and reshape their lenses, which grants them the capacity to restructure their realities.

So how exactly do we support students' emotional well-being? How do we empower them so they no longer feel like victims to outside circumstances? How do we inspire them to take control of their thoughts, feelings, and behaviors? To begin, we can acknowledge that "soft skills" are as important as "hard skills" and make the commitment to teach emotional intelligence in the classroom. We can explicitly teach happiness as a life skill that can be learned, strengthened, and maintained with conscious daily attention, emphasizing that happiness is a state of being, not a state of achieving. (See Happiness unit outline provided in back of book.) And, finally, we can reinforce the habit of optimism and introspection through daily "positivity practices" in the classroom. Ten years ago I started a daily reflective practice called "Birdseed" which began every class period and aimed to nourish students' souls as well as their minds. It was a ten minute character-building activity that involved group discussion and independent journaling on an inspirational quote. The routine was simple, but the results were so remarkable that I was moved to share it with other educators. Thus, this book was born. The daily activity addresses every facet of emotional intelligence and explicitly orients students' brains to consider and experience life from a more optimistic and healthy perspective.

Birdseed is a transformative tool ideal for any primary, middle, or high school setting. My hope is that it will be adopted as a daily practice in classrooms all over the world to create healthy cultures of joy, kindness, respect, curiosity, and self-awareness. Recognizing the ever-increasing demand for social-emotional learning and making the commitment to teach it is crucial in ensuring the enduring happiness AND success of our students.

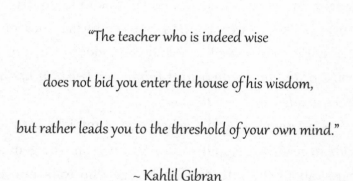

"The teacher who is indeed wise

does not bid you enter the house of his wisdom,

but rather leads you to the threshold of your own mind."

~ Kahlil Gibran

The Magic of Birdseed

Throughout my first several years of teaching, the pitiful stick-bird seen above was an endearing emblem on the whiteboard of every middle and high school classroom I taught in from Grand Junction, Colorado to Istanbul, Turkey. The bird became an enduring beacon of inspiration and served as a daily reminder to students that *some of the most important things we learn in life don't have grades attached to them.*

As a Language Arts teacher, one of my jobs is to teach kids to read, write, and speak. As a person who genuinely cares about the little human beings who walk into class every day, another one of my jobs is to nurture their souls and inspire them to think about who they are and who they want to become. Without doubt, I consider both responsibilities equally important. During my first year of teaching, I introduced an activity to start every class period that aimed to nourish students' spirits as well as their minds. It produced such remarkable results that I was moved to share it with other educators. The daily activity known as "Birdseed" involves 3–5 minutes of whole group discussion based on an inspirational quote followed by 3–4 minutes of independent journaling. While the practice itself is simple, the collective benefits are nothing less than extraordinary.

The routine and relevance of Birdseed is introduced at the beginning of every school year by sharing the parable below, which is my own exaggerated version of a joke shared with me years ago by veteran visionary and teacher extraordinaire John Wayne Schlatter (*aka* Jack). Jack passed away in December, 2014 after more than fifty years in education. He spent his last 14 years substitute teaching in Grand Junction, Colorado where he left behind an unprecedented legacy. He was beloved by students and revered by the teaching community, not as a master of any particular subject, but as a master of the art of teaching itself. He knew touching students' hearts by first making them *feel* and then making them *think* was the first step in leading them towards success. Jack was like a walking Hallmark card, full of inspirational anecdotes and motivational quotes. You couldn't pass the guy in the hallway without him stopping to pay you a compliment or share his latest one-liner. His emotional effect on others, particularly students, was more than powerful. It was transformational. Jack's spirit is immortal, living on in the halls of countless schools and ever-ingrained in the hearts of thousands of students. In his memory, it is my honor to share the story behind Birdseed:

> *One day there was a man who purchased a very exotic and expensive bird from a pet shop. The man took his new companion home and gave it everything he thought it could possibly need. He spared no expense and bought the bird a cage of the finest steel, and within it he placed silver bells, a golden mirror, and a hand carved wooden perch. The kind man quickly grew to love the bird, and every day he would talk to it for hours on end, sharing snippets of great truths and gems of worldly wisdom, believing that this time and attention would help it to live a long and happy life. One morning the man woke eager to greet his friend as he did at the start of every new day, but in the grand cage he found a most dreadful sight...The bird lay stretched, stone-cold, and still on the bottom. Heartsick and confused the man scooped up his lifeless friend and returned*

to the pet store to demand an explanation from the shop owner.

"How could this have happened?" he cried. "I did everything in the world for that bird! It had the most exquisite cage, expensive bells, a magnificent mirror, a one of a kind perch. I devoted my heart and soul to this bird. How in the world could it have died?"

The shop owner stared sadly at the man for a moment and then asked one simple question:

"Sir," he said gently, "did you give it birdseed?"

And with that we can see the grave mistake the bird's owner made. Despite sincere attempts to give his beloved friend everything he thought it needed, he neglected to provide the most fundamental necessity for growth and survival: food.

As a high school teacher, I find this story to be a great analogy for what happens—or doesn't happen—in the classroom. Metaphorically speaking, we provide students with all the bells and whistles of modern instruction, but then forget to *feed* them. With the best of intentions we impart what we hold to be the essentials of education, the core concepts of every subject matter, too often neglecting to acknowledge or address what *truly sustains students as human beings.* Seldom are we given the time, authority, or support to teach our kids about self-awareness, self-love, happiness, integrity, purpose, or compassion—and in turn, *we starve their souls.*

Birdseed is a tool that nourishes students' spirits as well as their minds, which ensures their growth as people, not just as pupils. Do motivational quotes and inspirational anecdotes truly have the power to influence a child's path or change a life? Absolutely. Neuroscientists and psychologists know that an optimistic mindset is a far greater indicator for happiness and success than any external factor. Therefore, by teaching students to retrain their brains with habituated patterns of positive thought, they create new neural pathways which allow them to see and experience more happiness and ultimately more opportunities for success.

Learning to structure the perfect essay in proper MLA format and finally figuring out what a participle is and why it's dangling are noteworthy skills, no doubt. But that isn't going to nourish the spirit or pull someone up off the floor in his darkest hour. It isn't going to give direction to the aimless soul who doesn't believe she has a purpose in this world. When our children are hungry for hope and searching for the light, remembering the difference between an independent and a dependent clause will be about as valuable as a sweater in the Sahara. We have to serve up something greater than the commonly prescribed curriculum and plant seeds of wisdom and faith that will give them strength in the years to come. Our personal standards as teachers must be higher because our kids desperately need the kind of nourishment that is seldom offered in mainstream instruction. The recipe for magic and growth in the classroom is incomplete without *all three* ingredients: *education, empowerment, and inspiration.*

The daily Birdseed activity bridges the gap between emotional intelligence and academic achievement. In addition to developing students' writing skills, it transforms the classroom atmosphere by strengthening relationships with and among students, fostering personal growth, improving communication, providing predictable daily structure, and creating a safe and nurturing environment. This multifaceted exchange serves as a foundation, and ultimately a springboard, for academic and personal success within and well beyond the classroom.

Building student-teacher relationships is the first step toward creating a solid foundation for students' personal growth and academic development. Beginning each day with whole-group discussions exploring matters of the heart and soul is something the kids look forward to and genuinely appreciate. They get to feel, think, and talk about concepts that are typically not addressed in school, and this sends the loud and clear message that who they are is as important as what they do. When our kids know they are seen, heard, and cared about as people, not just as students, they respond in kind, and the positive effects are reflected in their efforts and productivity in the classroom.

Daily conversations on concepts such as happiness, integrity, courage, self-respect, and gratitude promote critical thinking and cultivate self-awareness. As they explore these abstract ideas, they discover and share deeper shades of themselves with one another, which visibly reinforces the sense of community within the classroom. As students strengthen their intrapersonal and interpersonal skills, they solidify the fundamental foundation necessary to flourish intellectually, socially, and emotionally.

The journaling exercise that follows these conversations develops students' writing skills while building lines of communication that allow a private insight into their worlds. Students write in response to each quote daily for 3-4 minutes, and I collect their journals at the end of every week. I am endlessly amazed at how much I learn about my kids that I would otherwise never know. Within their reflections they share things about their present lives, their pasts, their dreams, and their struggles that help me to connect and communicate with them more effectively. I write little notes here and there, acknowledging their whispers to be heard, and this creates a tie that binds. When I return their journals, they immediately flip through the pages to find my comments and see that I have actually taken the time to read their words.

While reading through journals at the end of every week may seem like a time-consuming task added to an already demanding profession, it truly saves time in the end because students who feel cared for will give their full respect and attention in return, which means more class time can be spent on teaching and learning instead of redirecting negative behaviors and reteaching material.

In addition to strengthening writing skills, building relationships, improving communication, and fostering personal development, the daily practice of Birdseed provides a strong sense of structure and security, which is crucial to any primary, middle, or high school setting. One of the basics of behavior management is establishing predictable daily routines. Once this activity is introduced, chaotic transitions into class are virtually eliminated as students know exactly what they should be doing the second they walk through the door. They automatically look to the stick-bird on the board and the day's Birdseed written beneath it and follow the daily procedure: grab journal; copy quote; prepare to think, speak, and write. Furthermore, they know based on the nature of concepts discussed that their character and well-being is of the utmost importance, which makes them feel valued and protected.

Psychologist Abraham Maslow recognized that human behavior is motivated by a hierarchy of needs, and as teachers, we have to acknowledge this and act accordingly. We must address students' intrinsic needs as human beings first and foremost, remembering we are not merely teaching subjects—we are teaching children. Neuroscience has proven that emotion and cognition are interdependent, which, simply put, means the better students *feel*, the better they can *think*. Providing for their sense of safety, structure, and connection while crafting a platform for self-actualization must be considered a necessity, not an inconvenience or gratuitous effort.

It's important to note that research reflects one in four children have experienced—or are experiencing—some degree of significant trauma in their lives. This means a large majority of students walking through our doors every day are at a profound physiological disadvantage. If students are in crisis mode or aren't having their basic needs met outside of school, we can't realistically expect them to prioritize learning or reach their full potential when there's an internal lack of balance and stability. Severe or recurrent stress or trauma wires the brain to operate from the primitive survival mode, which adversely affects concentration, memory, and comprehension. Many students simply lack the capacity to perform as expected because they are living, however subconsciously, in fight or flight mode. This hypervigilant state also adversely affects their perceptions, experiences, and interactions with others and invariably manifests in the form of negative behaviors. Therefore, addressing the social-emotional domain and creating a warm and nurturing environment is as much a professional responsibility as it is an ethical endeavor.

The question is, how do we serve this particular population, especially when so many victims of trauma are "invisible" or unidentified? There is no single answer or solution, but one proactive step every teacher can take is to create an emotionally safe and healthy space for every student to grow. This in and of itself is therapeutic. The Birdseed activity works wonders for every demographic as it—quite literally—helps students to retrain their brains to think from a more positive perspective, which improves mood while increasing motivation, concentration, and productivity. Any student who is physically at ease is better able to focus his or her attention and regulate his or her behaviors in the classroom, so beginning each class period with a calming procedure that sets a positive tone is advantageous for everyone.

As educators we must actively commit to addressing the social-emotional domain as fervently as we do any other. Focusing solely on academic achievement without addressing emotional intelligence is an incomplete and unbalanced approach to education. Students' psychological health—their self-concepts, their perceptions of the world, their levels of resilience, their interpersonal capacities—form the foundation on which all else is built. If this internal infrastructure is weak, life-long struggles will inevitably ensue, and no amount of scholarly savvy can compensate for such deficiency. Knowledge of subjects without knowledge of Self does not orient students for happiness or adequately prepare them for success or life's inescapable challenges. Therefore, students need thoughtful, consistent, and direct instruction to develop the skills, attitudes, and values necessary to thrive.

Do we have time to teach emotional intelligence in the classroom? The answer is simple: We must *make* the time. In the words of Dr. Martin Luther King Jr.: "Intelligence plus character—that is the goal of true education." If that's not the goal, we're missing the big picture. Exploring what makes us human, empowering students with self-knowledge and life skills, and planting seeds of inspiration is directly related to fostering academic achievement. This is what it means to engage students in an authentic learning process. Teaching is both an art and a science, and the magic made in the classroom is an alchemy all its own.

At the beginning of every school year, I share the story about the man and his bird, and the students immediately recognize and appreciate the parallel between the story and the daily practice of Birdseed. They are genuinely moved, and often shocked, to hear that their character development means as much—if not more—than anything else, and this is where their journeys toward greatness begin. Share the story of Birdseed in your own words; commit to feeding students' souls along with their minds, and wait for the magic to unfold. Your young fledglings will participate in the daily practice with endearing enthusiasm, and you'll watch as your classroom environment transforms into a fertile breeding ground for happiness and success.

"All of your scholarship, all of your study of Shakespeare and Wordsworth would be in vain if at the same time you did not build your character and attain mastery over your thoughts and your actions."

~ Mahatma Gandhi

"Knowing is not enough; we must apply.

Willing is not enough; we must do."

~ Johann Wolfgang von Goethe

Using Birdseed in the Classroom

Countless hours have been spent in the early morning light of my classrooms searching the internet for the perfect quotes to spark powerful conversations. There are—literally—millions of quotes to sort through on the internet (and other countless resources), but included here are the few shiny gems (365) that have served time and again as catalysts for remarkable dialogue. Some have made students laugh; some have instigated healthy debates; some have temporarily left them confused, but all have made them think.

The quotes are organized according to concepts, and many are metaphorical as I believe we learn best and remember most through metaphors. I have also made every effort to give credit where it's due by including a brief biographical snippet about each contributor in the index, should you decide to share this. Often, learning about the lives of these visionaries serves as a lesson in itself.

There are several ways you can put Birdseed into practice. You might randomly choose a daily quote for discussion and written reflection, or you can choose a quote based on its theme and relate it to curriculum you are currently studying. Allowing a different student each day to open the book to a random page and choose a "message from the universe" is also a fun way to get the kids involved.

I prefer to have Birdseed written on the board before students walk into class, which makes for a calm, smooth transition. They enter the room, grab their journals, look to the stick-bird on the board and begin copying the quote. This gives me a few peaceful minutes to take attendance and gear up for the lesson ahead.

Once everyone has written down the day's Birdseed, I start asking questions to generate discussion. (After this procedure has been in place for a while, you'll see the hands start flying up before you even prompt them.) After reading the day's quote aloud, I ask questions like:

> *What does this mean?*
> *What does this remind you of?*
> *Do you agree or disagree?*
> *How might this be true?*
> *How might this be a metaphor for life?*
> *How does this apply to you?*

Students are always more than eager to share their thoughts and connections, and after 3–4 minutes of whole group discussion, followed by my own thoughts on the quote, they are able to write independently on the topic with ease for 2–3 minutes. When there's time, I let a few share their reflections with the class.

Allowing students the opportunity to lead the Birdseed activity on occasion is a fabulous idea. In my classroom, every Friday I offer the spotlight to a student who can choose his or her own quote, write it on the board, and lead the whole-group discussion. They enjoy this so much they practically argue over the chance to do it, so to avoid conflict, I randomly draw a name out of a jar at the beginning of each week.

*Accommodations: Students with exceptional needs may benefit from having the daily quotes already written down for them. If they struggle with the first step of copying Birdseed from the board in a timely manner, they have less time to think about the meaning behind it and miss out on the opportunity to participate in discussion. For these students, it's a good idea to have the day's (or the week's) Birdseed typed up and discreetly placed in their journals, which are always left in the classroom. Then, they can focus their attention on the discussion and written reflections.

At the end of every week, I collect students' journals and read through their entries, always making an effort to write thoughtful comments in response to at least one of their reflections so they feel validated. I never grade their mechanics or grammar, as I don't want the flow of their thoughts interrupted by the fear of criticism. Instead, I give "completion" or "participation" points, which factor into their final grades.

Obviously, you can shorten, stretch, or alter this activity however you choose to make it work best for you and your students. This is simply one more tool to add to your box of tricks that will hopefully leave you as inspired as those you share it with.

However you choose to use Birdseed, I commend you for your commitment and devotion to the Higher Calling of educating, empowering, and inspiring the world's children.

In the words of Zig Ziglar: "Motivation doesn't last. Neither does bathing. That's why we recommend it daily."

Let the magic begin...

Character & Integrity

"You can easily judge the character of a man by how he treats those who can do nothing for him."
~ Malcolm S. Forbes

***

"Nearly all men can stand adversity, but if you want to test a man's character, give him power."
~ Abraham Lincoln

***

"It is better to be hated for what you are than loved for what you are not."
~ Andre Gide

"Adversity will do something to you or for you..."
~ Napoleon Hill

***

"What you do speaks so loudly that I cannot hear what you say."
~ Ralph Waldo Emerson

***

"We are what we repeatedly do. Excellence, then, is not an act, but a habit."
~ Aristotle

***

"I speak to everyone in the same way, whether he is the garbage man or the president of the university."
~ Albert Einstein

"You must be the change you wish to see in the world."
~ *Mahatma Gandhi*

***

"To believe in something and not to live it is dishonest."
~ *Mahatma Gandhi*

***

"Smooth seas do not make skillful sailors."
~ *African Proverb*

***

"No one can make you feel inferior without your consent."
~ *Eleanor Roosevelt*

"When something bad happens, you have three choices: You can let it define you, let it destroy you, or you can let it strengthen you."

~ Unknown

***

"If only people would realize that moral principles are like measles...They have to be caught. And only the people who've got them can pass on the contagion."

~ John Adams

***

"Watch your thoughts. They become words. Watch your words. They become deeds. Watch your deeds. They become habits. They become character. Character is everything."

~ Ralph Waldo Emerson

"Great spirits have always encountered violent opposition from mediocre minds."
~ *Albert Einstein*

***

"Happiness is when what you think, what you say, and what you do are in harmony."
~ *Mahatma Gandhi*

***

"All of your scholarship, all your study of Shakespeare and Wordsworth would be vain if at the same time you did not build your character and attain mastery over your thoughts and your actions."
~ *Mahatma Gandhi*

***

"Know thyself."
~ *Socrates*

"It's better to stand alone and be right than stand with millions and be wrong."

~ Unknown

***

"The finest steel is forged through the hottest fires."

~ Unknown

***

"Be not afraid of greatness. Some are born great, some achieve greatness, and others have greatness thrust upon them."

~ William Shakespeare

***

"It is our choices that show who we truly are far more than our abilities."

~ JK Rowling

"In the end, we will remember not the words of our enemies, but the silence of our friends."
~ MLK Jr

***

"You were born an original. Don't die a copy."
~ John Mason

***

"To be yourself in a world that is constantly trying to make you something else is the greatest accomplishment."
~ Henry David Thoreau

***

"The shoe that fits one person pinches another; there is no recipe for living that suits all cases."
~ Carl Jung

"Be more concerned with your character than with your reputation. Your character is what you really are, while your reputation is merely what others think you are."

~ John Wooden

***

"Character cannot be developed in ease and quiet. Only through experience of trial and suffering can the soul be strengthened, ambition inspired, and success achieved."

~ Hellen Keller

***

"There is no better test of a man's integrity than his behavior when he is wrong."

~ Marvin Williams

"It is what a man thinks of himself that determines his fate."

~ Henry David Thoreau

***

"We are what we pretend to be, so we must be careful about what we pretend to be."

~ Kurt Vonnegut

***

"It is better to fail in originality than to succeed in imitation."

~ Herman Melville

***

"I have yet to meet a man as fond of high moral conduct as he is of outward appearances."

~ Confucius

"We should be too big to take offense and too noble to give it."

~ Abraham Lincoln

***

"Tolerance implies a gratuitous assumption of the inferiority of other faiths to one's own."

~ Mahatma Gandhi

***

"Judging others says more about your character than it does theirs."

~ Unknown

***

"Our character is defined by what we do when we think no one is looking."

~ H. Jackson Brown

"Character, like a photograph, develops in
darkness."
~ Yousuf Karsh

***

"Character, not the circumstances, makes the
person."
~ Booker T. Washington

***

"It's not how we make mistakes, but how we correct
them that defines us."
~ Unknown

***

"Be the type of person who leaves a mark, not a
scar."
~ Unknown

"If you're always trying to be normal, you'll never know how amazing you can be."

~ Maya Angelo

***

"Decisions are so much easier to make when you know what your values are."

~ Unknown

***

"Taking responsibility for your beliefs and judgements gives you the power to change them."

~ Byron Katie

***

"A man's character may be learned from the adjectives which he habitually uses in conversation."

~ Mark Twain

Compassion

"Compassion and tolerance are not a sign of
weakness, but a sign of strength."
~ Dalai Lama

***

"Until he extends the circle of his compassion to all
living things, man himself will not find peace."
~ Albert Schweitzer

***

"Men are only as great as they are kind."
~ Elbert Hubbard

"No act of kindness, no matter how small, is ever wasted."

~ Aesop

***

"If your compassion does not include yourself, it is incomplete."

~ Buddha

***

"Those who are the hardest to love need it the most."

~ Socrates

***

"If you don't like someone, make it a point to know him better."

~ Abraham Lincoln

"If you have to choose between being right and being kind, choose being kind, and you will always be right."

~ Wayne Dyer

***

"Be kind, for everyone you meet is fighting a battle you know nothing about."

~ Wendy Mass

***

"The noblest way to use your voice is to speak for those who don't have one. All animals deserve to be heard."

~ Anam Cara Cat

Courage & Determination

"Great spirits have always encountered violent
opposition from mediocre minds."
~ Albert Einstein

***

"The greater danger for most of us lies not in setting
our aim too high and falling short, but in setting our
aim too low and achieving our mark."
~ Michelangelo

"Courage is not the absence of fear, but rather the strength to press forward despite it."
~ Ralph Waldo Emerson

***

"It's easy to stand with the crowd. It takes courage to stand alone."
~ Mahatma Gandhi

***

"Man cannot discover new oceans unless he has the courage to lose sight of the shore."
~ Andre Gide

***

"The only impossible journey is the one you never begin."
~ Tony Robbins

"Seek opportunity, not security. A boat in the harbor is safe, but in time its bottom will rot out."

~ H. Jackson Brown Jr

***

"Every adversity, every failure, every heartache carries with it the seed of an equal or greater benefit."

~ Napoleon Hill

***

"You can't fall if you don't climb. But there's no joy in living your whole life on the ground."

~ Unknown

***

"There is nothing in a caterpillar that tells you it's going to be a butterfly."

~ Buckminster Fuller

"Little minds are tamed and subdued by misfortune–but great minds rise above them."
~ *Washington Irving*

***

"There is only one way to avoid criticism: Do nothing, say nothing, and be nothing."
~ *Aristotle*

***

"Two roads diverged in a wood, and I took the one less traveled by, and that has made all the difference."
~ *Robert Frost*

***

"Courage doesn't always roar. Sometimes courage is the little voice at the end of the day that says I'll try again tomorrow."
~ *Mary Anne Radmacher*

"I have not failed. I've just found 10,000 ways that won't work."
~ *Thomas Edison*

***

"When it's obvious that the goals cannot be reached, don't adjust the goals; adjust the action steps."
~ *Confucius*

***

"Don't be afraid to go out on a limb; that's where the fruit is."
~ *Unknown*

***

"There are two primary choices in life: to accept conditions as they exist, or accept the responsibility for changing them."
~ *Denis Waitly*

"Snowflakes are one of nature's most fragile things, but just look at what they can do when they stick together."
~ Vista M. Kelly

***

"Most of the important things in the world have been accomplished by people who have kept on trying when there seemed to be no hope at all."
~ Dale Carnegie

***

"You must expect great things of yourself before you can do them."
~ Michael Jordan

***

"Every accomplishment in reality began as a dream in the clouds."
~ Anam Cara Cat

"People who are crazy enough to think they can change the world are the ones who do."

~ Rob Siltanen

***

"Keep away from people who try to belittle your dreams. Small people always do that, but the really great ones make you feel that you too, can become great."

~ Mark Twain

***

"Shoot for the moon. Even if you miss, you'll land among the stars."

~ Brian Littrell

***

"It's never too late to be what you might have been."

~ George Eliot

"It is what a man thinks of himself that really determines his fate."
~ *Henry David Thoreau*

***

"Do not go where the path may lead; go instead where there is no path and leave a trail."
~ *Ralph Waldo Emerson*

***

"Only those who risk going too far can ever possibly know how far one can go."
~ *T.S. Elliot*

***

"Great works are performed not by strength but by perseverance."
~ Samuel Johnson

"People of accomplishment rarely sit back and let things happen to them; they go out and happen to things."
~ Leonardo DaVinci

***

"Whatever you can do or dream you can, begin it. Boldness has beauty, power, and magic in it."
~ Johann Wolfgang Von Goethe

***

"The first step towards getting somewhere is to decide you're not going to stay where you are."
~ J.P. Morgan

***

"Our greatest glory is not in never falling, but in rising every time we fall."
~ Confucius

"The strongest people aren't always the people who win, but they're the people who don't give up when they lose."

~ Ashley Hodgeson

***

"It takes a certain kind of courage not to settle, and it takes a special kind of strength to admit you have. Sometimes walking away is the bravest thing you can do."

~ Anam Cara Cat

***

"If one advances confidently in the direction of one's dreams, and endeavors to live the life which one has imagined, he will meet with a success unexpected in common hours."

~ Henry David Thoreau

"Sometimes giving up isn't really giving up; it's just changing your mind."

~ Anam Cara Cat

***

"The difference between a successful person and others is not a lack of strength, not a lack of knowledge, but rather a lack in will."

~ Vince Lombardi

***

"Fairy tales are more than true: not because they tell us that dragons exist, but because they tell us that dragons can be beaten."

~ Neil Gaiman

***

"Decide what to be and go be it."

~ Scott Avett

Faith

"Faith is taking the first step even when you don't
see the whole staircase."
~ Martin Luther King Jr.

***

"Everything will be okay in the end. If it's not okay,
it's not the end."
~ John Lennon

***

"To accomplish great things, we must not only act,
but also dream, not only plan, but also believe."
~ Anatole France

"Worry is simply having faith in the wrong thing."
~ *Ralph Waldo Emerson*

***

"Leap and the net will appear."
~ *John Burroughs*

***

"Sometimes our fate resembles a fruit tree in winter.
Who would think those branches would turn green
again and blossom? But we hope; we know it."
~ *Johann Wolfgang van Goethe*

***

"Remember that sometimes not getting what you
want is a wonderful stroke of luck."
~ *Dalai Lama*

"You'll see it when you believe it."
~ *Wayne Dyer*

***

"Follow your bliss and don't be afraid, and doors will open where you didn't know they were going to be."
~ *Joseph Campbell*

***

"Once you make a decision, the universe conspires to make it happen."
~ *Ralph Waldo Emerson*

***

"People don't always get what they deserve, but they usually get what they expect. Think big. Expect the extraordinary."
~ *Anam Cara Cat*

"Sometimes the wrong train takes us to the right
place."
~ *Paulo Coelho*

****

"If we knew how everything was going to play out,
there'd be no need for faith, no call upon the gods,
and nothing epic about the adventure. There is
magic in uncertainty. Of that you can be certain."
~ *Anam Cara Cat*

***

"I have learned that faith means trusting in advance
what will only make sense in reverse."
~ *Phillip Yancey*

***

"Feed only your faith and your doubts will starve."
~ *Unknown*

Forgiveness

"An eye for an eye leaves the whole world blind."
~ Mahatma Gandhi

***

"Holding onto anger is like grasping a hot coal with the intent of throwing it at someone else; you are the one who gets burned."
~ Buddha

***

"Holding onto anger is like drinking poison and expecting the other person to die."
~ Unknown

"The weak can never forgive. Forgiveness is an attribute of the strong."
~ *Mahatma Gandhi*

***

"Forgiveness does not change the past, but it does enlarge the future."
~ *Paul Boese*

***

"Conflict cannot survive without your participation."
~ *Wayne Dyer*

***

"You will not be punished for your anger; you will be punished by your anger."
~ *Buddha*

***

"For every minute you're angry you lose sixty seconds of happiness."
~ *Ralph Waldo Emerson*

"Getting over a painful experience is much like crossing the monkey bars; you have to let go at some point in order to move on."

~ C.S. Lewis

***

"Am I not destroying my enemies when I make friends of them?"

~ Abraham Lincoln

***

"When you forgive, you are in no way changing the past, but you sure are changing the future."

~ Bernard Meltzer

***

"Forgive others not because they deserve it, but because you deserve peace."

~ Jonathan Lockwood Huie

Gratitude

"Do not spoil what you have by desiring what you have not; remember that what you now have was once among the things you only hoped for."

~ Epicurus

***

"Feeling gratitude has less to do with what you have and more to do with how you look at what you have. Therefore, how much you have to be grateful for is entirely up to you."

~ Anam Cara Cat

"The more you appreciate your blessings the more blessings you'll have to appreciate."
~ Anam Cara Cat

***

"Feeling gratitude and not expressing it is like wrapping a present and not giving it."
~ William Arthur Ward

***

"The only people with whom you should try to get even are those who have helped you."
~ John E. Southard

***

"Silent gratitude isn't much use to anyone."
~ G.B. Stern

"Enjoy the little things, for one day you may look back and realize they were the big things."

~ Robert Brault

***

"You have been given a gift of 84,600 seconds today. Have you used one of them to say thank you?"

~ William Arthur Ward

***

"It's not happy people who are grateful. It's grateful people who are happy."

~ Unknown

***

"Be thankful for what you have. Your life, no matter how bad you think it is, is someone else's fairy tale."

~ Wale Ayeni

"If a fellow isn't thankful for what he's got, he isn't likely to be thankful for what he's going to get."
~ Frank A. Clark

***

"We often take for granted the very things that most deserve our gratitude."
~ Cynthia Ozick

***

"Gratitude is an art of painting adversity into a lovely picture."
~ Kak Sri

***

"He is a wise man who does not grieve for the things which he has not, but rejoices for those which he has."
~ Epictetus

"Not what we say about our blessings, but how we use them, is the true measure of our thanksgiving."

~ W.T. Purkiser

***

"There is no greater difference between men than between grateful and ungrateful people."

~ R.H. Blyth

***

"If you want to feel rich, just count the things you have that money cannot buy."

~ Unknown

***

"He who is not contented with what he has would not be contented with what he would like to have."

~ Socrates

"Gratitude is the healthiest of all human emotions. The more you express gratitude for what you have, the more likely you will have even more to express gratitude for."
~ Zig Ziglar

***

"Sometimes we should express our gratitude for the small and simple things like the scent of the rain, the taste of your favorite food, or the sound of a loved one's voice."
~ Joseph B. Wirthlin

***

"If we cannot alleviate others' suffering, the very least we can do is honor it by acknowledging–and appreciating–the many blessings we take for granted."
~ Anam Cara Cat

"Gratitude is a mark of a noble soul and a refined character. We like to be around those who are grateful."
~ *Joseph B. Wirthlin*

***

"Social scientists have found that the fastest way to feel happiness is to practice gratitude."
~ *Chip Conley*

***

"Happiness isn't always the result of getting what we want. More often it's the result of appreciating what we already have."
~ *Unknown*

***

"Never underestimate the power of 'thank you.'"
~ *Anam Cara Cat*

Passion

"Don't ask what the world needs; ask what makes you come alive and go do it because what the world needs is more people who have come alive."
~ Howard Thurman

***

"Once you have tasted flight, you will forever walk the earth with your eyes turned skyward, for there you have been and there you will always long to return."
~ Leonardo da Vinci

"The tragedy of life is not that it ends so soon, but that we wait so long to begin it."

~ W.M. Lewis

***

"I never did a day's work in my life. It was all fun."

~ Thomas A. Edison

***

"If it's important to you, you'll find a way. If not, you'll find an excuse."

~ Unknown

***

"Twenty years from now you'll be more disappointed by the things you didn't do than by the ones you did do. Sail away from the safe harbor. Explore. Dream. Discover."

~ Mark Twain

"Nothing great was ever achieved without enthusiasm."
~ *Henry David Thoreau*

***

"You're alive only once, as far as we know, and what could be worse than getting to the end of your life and realizing you hadn't lived it?"
~ *Edward Albee*

***

"My mission in life is not merely to survive, but to thrive, and to do so with some passion, some compassion, some humor, and some style."
~ *Maya Angelou*

***

"Don't wait for extraordinary opportunities. Seize common occasions and make them great."
~ *Orison Swett Marden*

"Every great dream begins with a dreamer. Always remember, you have within you the strength, the patience, and the passion to reach for the stars to change the world."

~ Harriet Tubman

***

"There is no passion to be found in playing small—in settling for a life that is less than the one you are capable of living."

~ Nelson Mandela

***

"Great ambition is the passion of a great character. Those endowed with it may perform very good or very bad acts. All depends on the principles which direct them."

~ Napoleon Bonaparte

"Carpe diem!"

~ Horace

***

"The second you allow others to determine the value of your gift, your divine talent becomes a cheap commodity."

~ Anam Cara Cat

***

"If we spent half as much energy following our bliss as we do chasing after misery, we'd never be lost again."

~ Anam Cara Cat

***

"Never doubt that a single person can change the world; indeed it's the only thing that ever has."

~ Margaret Mead

Perspective & Positive Thinking

"People often say that motivation doesn't last. Well, neither does bathing. That's why we recommend it daily."

~ Zig Ziglar

***

"When one door closes, another opens, but we often look so long and regretfully at the closed door that we do not see the one which has opened for us."

~ Alexander Graham Bell

"The outer conditions of a person's life will always be found to reflect his inner beliefs."

~ James Allen

***

"The pessimist complains about the wind; the optimist expects it to change; the realist adjusts the sails."

~ William Arthur Ward

***

"The game of life is a game of boomerangs. Our thoughts, deeds, and words return to us sooner or later with astounding accuracy."

~ Florence Scovel Shin

***

"What we think, we become."

~ Buddha

"The pessimist sees difficulty in every opportunity;
an optimist sees opportunity in every difficulty."
~ Winston Churchill

***

"An obstacle is merely a stepping stone."
~ William Prescott

***

"In the long run, the pessimist may be proven right,
but the optimist has a better time on the trip."
~ Daniel L. Reardon

***

"Life is ten percent what happens to you and ninety
percent how you look at it."
~ Lou Holtz

"Don't cry because it's over. Smile because it happened."

~ Dr. Seuss

***

"Whether you think you can or think you can't, either way you are right."

~ Henry Ford

***

"Don't let life discourage you. Everyone who got where he is had to start where he was."

~ Richard L. Evans

***

"A mind is like a parachute. It doesn't work if it isn't open."

~ Frank Zappa

"What the caterpillar calls the end of the world, the butterfly calls a beginning."
~ Richard Bach

***

"All the world's a stage, and all the men and women merely players; they have their exits and their entrances, and one man in his time plays many parts."
~ William Shakespeare

***

"Magic works kind of like a vampire—you have to invite it in."
~ Anam Cara Cat

***

"Your imagination is your preview of life's coming attractions."
~ Albert Einstein

"I can choose either to be a victim of the world or an adventurer in search of treasure. It's all a question of how I view my life."

~ Paulo Coelho

***

"Life is not about waiting for the storm to pass. It's about learning how to dance in the rain."

~ Vivian Greene

***

"There are two ways to live your life: You can live as if nothing is a miracle or you can live as if everything is a miracle."

~ Albert Einstein

***

"You become what you think about."

~ Napoleon Hill

"I've lived through some terrible things in my life, some of which actually happened."
~ Mark Twain

***

"I would rather live in a world where my life is surrounded by mystery than live in a world so small that my mind could comprehend it."
~ Henry Emerson Fosdick

***

"Life is 10% what happens to me and 90% how I react to it."
~ Charles Swindoll

***

"Those who don't believe in magic will never find it."
~ Roald Dahl

"It's not what you look at that matters; it's what you see."

~ Henry David Thoreau

***

"The mind is its own place and in itself can make a heaven of hell or a hell of heaven."

~ John Milton

***

"If the stars should appear but one night every thousand years how man would marvel and stare."

~ Ralph Waldo Emerson

***

"There are no failures, just experiences and your reactions to them."

~ Tom Krause

"There can't be a happy ending to an unhappy journey."

~ Ester Hicks

***

"We do not see things as they are. We see things as we are."

~ Anais Nin

***

"All that we are is the result of what we have thought. The mind is everything. What we think we become."

~ Buddha

***

"Change the way you look at things and the things you look at will change."

~ Wayne Dyer

"There is a huge amount of freedom that comes to you when you take nothing personally."

~ Don Miguel Ruiz

***

"The deeper that sorrow carves into your being, the more joy you can contain."

~ Kahlil Gibran

***

"There is no right or wrong. Only thinking makes it so."

~ William Shakespeare

***

"Positive thinking will let you do everything better than negative thinking will."

~ Zig Ziglar

"If you don't like something, change it. If you can't change it, change the way you think about it."

~ Mary Engelbreit

***

"When you complain about something, you double it. When you laugh at it, you destroy it."

~ Confucius

***

"Nurture your mind with great thoughts for you will never go any higher than you think."

~ Benjamin Disraeli

***

"A bad attitude is like a flat tire. If you don't change it, you'll never go anywhere."

~ Unknown

"The quality of your life depends on the quality of your thoughts."
~ *Marcus Aurelius*

***

"Dwelling on the negative only contributes to its power."
~ *Shirley MacLaine*

***

"We are all faced with a series of great opportunities brilliantly disguised as impossible situations."
~ *Charles R. Swindoll*

***

"You don't always get what you deserve, but you usually get what you expect. When you anticipate the extraordinary, you invite it into your life."
~ *Anam Cara Cat*

"What appear as roadblocks to success are often stepping stones in disguise."

~ Anam Cara Cat

***

"Your life is your greatest work of art. Like an abstract painting, some won't get it, some won't see the beauty in it, and some will tell you you've done it all wrong. But every artist knows that with a change in light, everything looks different."

~ Anam Cara Cat

***

"Acknowledging there are some things we have control over and some things we don't—and recognizing the difference between the two—is the ultimate state of freedom."

~ Anam Cara Cat

"Where we come from doesn't define who we are or determine where we end up. Victim or victor—either way, it's a choice."
~ Anam Cara Cat

***

"Optimism is the one quality more associated with happiness and success than any other."
~ Brian Tracy

***

"Everything we hear is opinion, not fact. Everything we see is perspective, not truth."
~ Marcus Aurelius

***

"Happiness is to be found along the way, not at the end of the road, for then the journey is over and it's too late."
~ R. Updegraff

"If you knew how powerful your thoughts are, you would never have a negative thought again."

~ Peace Pilgrim"

***

"Don't let negative and toxic people rent space in your head. Raise the rent and kick them out."

~ Robin Sharma

***

"Negative thinking is a habit. Positive thinking is a habit. Which one are you reinforcing?"

~ Anam Cara Cat

***

"It's not reality that shapes us, but rather the lens through which your brain views the world that shapes your reality."

~ Shawn Achor

Self-love & Self-respect

"Keep away from people who try to belittle your ambitions. Small people always do that, but the really great make you feel that you, too, can become great."

~ Mark Twain

***

"As we let our own light shine we unconsciously give other people permission to do the same."

~ Marianne Williamson

"Be strong enough to let go of what no longer serves you and patient enough to wait for what you deserve."
~ Unknown

***

"Never apologize for having high standards. People who really want to be in your life will rise up to meet them."
~ Ziad K. Abdelnour

***

"Your playing small does not serve the world. There is nothing enlightened about shrinking so that other people won't feel insecure around you."
~ Marianne Williamson

***

"Your value doesn't decrease based on someone's inability to see your worth."

~ Unknown

***

"You yourself as much as anybody in the entire universe deserve your love and affection."

~ Mahatma Gandhi

***

"Don't chase people. Be yourself, do your own thing and work hard. The right people—the ones who belong in your life—will come to you and stay."

~ Will Smith

***

"Never allow someone to be your priority while allowing yourself to be their option."

~ Mark Twain

"You cannot be lonely if you like the person you're alone with."

~ Wayne Dyer

***

"Be nice to yourself. It's hard to be happy when someone is mean to you all the time."

~ Christine Arlo

***

"When you dare to stand out, to think or do differently, you will either invoke admiration or provoke disapproval. The beauty of living authentically is you needn't be concerned with either one."

~ Anam Cara Cat

***

"You teach people how to treat you."

~ Unknown

"If there are chapters of your life that others find unacceptable or unappealing, it doesn't mean your pages are riddled with errors; it just might mean they don't belong in your story."

~ Anam Cara Cat

***

"The way you treat yourself sets the standards for others."

~ Sonia Friedman

***

"We romanticize the idea of finding someone else to 'complete us,' but incomplete people just attract more incomplete people. Sharing emptiness with someone else doesn't make it go away; it just gives you someone to blame it on."

~ Anam Cara Cat

Service & Contribution

"Not everybody can be famous, but everybody can be great because greatness is determined by service."

~ Martin Luther King Jr.

***

"You will achieve the greatest results in life if you replace the word 'achievement' with contribution."

~ Peter Drucker

"You cannot do a kindness too soon because you never know how soon it will be too late."
~ Ralph Waldo Emerson

***

"I have been impressed with the urgency of doing. Knowing is not enough; we must apply. Being willing is not enough; we must do."
~ Wolfgang von Goethe

***

"In the end, we will remember not the words of our enemies, but the silence of our friends."
~ Martin Luther King Jr.

***

"If you can't feed one hundred people, just feed one."
~ Mother Teresa

"How wonderful is it that nobody need wait a single moment before starting to improve the world."

~ Anne Frank

***

"The smallest act of kindness is worth more than the greatest intention."

~ Kahlil Gibran

***

"If you can't do great things, do small things in a great way."

~ Napoleon Hill

***

"There are two ways of spreading the light: to be the candle or the mirror that reflects it."

~ Edith Wharton

"I've learned that people will forget what you said, people will forget what you did, but people will never forget how you made them feel.

~ Maya Angelou

***

"Lighthouses don't go running all over an island looking for boats to save; they just stand there shining."

~ Anne Lamott

***

"I alone cannot change the world, but I can cast a stone across the waters to create many ripples."

~ Mother Teresa

***

"We all die. The goal isn't to live forever; the goal is to create something that will."

~ Chuck Palahniuk

"You have not lived a perfect day until you have done something for someone who cannot repay you."

~ John Wooden

***

"Don't judge each day by the harvest you reap, but by the seeds you plant."

~ Robert Louis Stevenson

***

"Often, our deepest wounds give birth to our greatest purpose."

~ Anam Cara Cat

***

"The best way to find yourself is to lose yourself in the service to others."

~ Mahatma Gandhi

Success

"The time will never be 'just right.' Start where you stand, and work with whatever tools you may have at your command, and better tools will be found as you go along."

~ Napoleon Hill

***

"Optimism is the one quality more associated with success and happiness than any other."

~ Brian Tracy

"Goals are like magnets. They'll attract the things that make them come true."
~ *Anthony Robbins*

***

"The road to success is always under construction."
~ *Arnold Palmer*

***

"A goal is a dream with a deadline."
~ *Napoleon Hill*

***

"Success is not the key to happiness. Happiness is the key to success. If you love what you are doing, you'll be a success."
~ *Albert Schweitzer*

"If you want to increase your success rate, double your failure rate."

~ Thomas J. Watson

***

"The secret to getting ahead is getting started."

~ Mark Twain

***

"Luck is what happens when preparation meets opportunity."

~ Seneca

***

"Don't wait. The time will never be just right."

~ Napoleon Hill

"Most great people have attained their greatest success just one step beyond their greatest failure."
~ Napoleon Hill

***

"Every great leader, from the dawn of civilization down to the present, was a dreamer."
~ Napoleon Hill

***

"If opportunity doesn't knock, build a door."
~ Milton Berle

***

"Whatever the mind can conceive and believe, it can achieve."
~ Napoleon Hill

"You miss 100% of the shots you don't take."
~ *Wayne Gretzky*

***

"The best time to plant a tree was 20 years ago. The second best time is now."
~ *Chinese proverb*

***

"The journey of a thousand miles begins with one step."
~ *Lao Tzu*

***

"To laugh often and much; to win the respect of intelligent people and the affection of children; to leave the world a better place; to know even one life has breathed easier because you have lived. This is to have succeeded."
~ *Ralph Waldo Emerson*

"Success is subjective. You get to define it; therefore you get to decide what determines your own level."
~ Unknown

***

"The starting point of all achievement is DESIRE."
~ Napoleon Hill

***

"Discontent is the first necessity of progress."
~ Thomas A. Edison

***

"If you have built castles in the air, your work need not be lost; that is where they should be. Now put the foundations under them."
~ Henry David Thoreau

"If you do what you've always done, you'll get what you've always gotten."

~ *Henry Ford*

***

"Bloom where you are planted."

~ *Proverb*

***

"Good fortune often happens when opportunity meets with preparation."

~ *Thomas A. Edison*

***

"Choose a job you love, and you will never have to work a day in your life."

~ *Confucius*

"It is better to fail in originality than to succeed in imitation."

~ Herman Melville

***

"It's not what we do once in a while that shapes our lives. It's what we do consistently."

~ Tony Robbins

***

"Many of life's failures are people who did not realize how close they were to success when they gave up."

~ Thomas A. Edison

***

"If you don't go after what you want, you'll never have it. If you don't ask, the answer is always no. If you don't step forward, you're always in the same place."

~ Nora Roberts

"Success will never be a big step in the future; success is a small step taken just now."
~ *Jonatan Mårtensson*

***

"A person who never made a mistake never tried anything new."
~ *Albert Einstein*

***

"The person who says it cannot be done should not interrupt the person who is doing it."
~ *Chinese proverb*

***

"I have not failed. I've just found 10,000 ways that won't work."
~ *Thomas Edison*

"Leaders spend 5% of their time on a problem and
95% on a solution."
~ *Anthony Robbins*

***

"Anyone who has never made a mistake has never
tried anything new."
~ *Albert Einstein*

***

"Life isn't about finding yourself. Life is about
creating yourself."
~ *George Bernard Shaw*

***

"The flower that blooms in adversity is the rarest
and most beautiful of all."
~ *Walt Disney Company*

"I can't change the direction of the wind, but I can adjust my sails to always reach my destination."
~ *Jimmy Dean*

***

"They succeed because they think they can."
~ *Virgil*

***

"Nobody can go back and start a new beginning, but anyone can start today and make a new ending."
~ *Maria Robinson*

***

"The greatest difference between successful people and unsuccessful people is not knowledge or talent, but degrees of discipline."
~ *Anam Cara Cat*

"A successful man is one who can lay a firm foundation with the bricks life has thrown at him."
~ David Brinkley

***

"Success is to be measured not so much by the position that one has reached in life as by the obstacles which he has overcome."
~ Booker T. Washington

***

"The foundation stones for a balanced success are honesty, character, integrity, faith, love, and loyalty."
~ Zig Ziglar

***

"If people aren't laughing at your dreams, your dreams aren't big enough."
~ Grayson Marshall

"The most important single ingredient in the formula of success is knowing how to get along with people."
~ *Theodore Roosevelt*

***

"Develop success from failures. Discouragement and failure are two of the surest stepping stones to success."
~ *Dale Carnegie*

***

"What's money? A man is a success if he gets up in the morning and goes to bed at night and in between does what he wants to."
~ *Bob Dylan*

***

"There is no failure except in no longer trying."
~ *Elbert Hubbard*

"If you want to succeed, you should strike out on new paths, rather than travel the worn paths of accepted success."
~ *John Rockefeller*

***

"Success is a state of mind. If you want success, you have to start thinking of yourself as a success."
~ *Dr. Joyce Brothers*

***

"A true measure of your worth includes all the benefits others have gained from your success."
~ *Cullen Hightower*

***

"Success is achieved by developing our strengths, not by eliminating our weaknesses."
~ *Marilyn Vos Savant*

"Ancient rule of 21: If you do anything for 21 days, it will be installed as a habit."

~ Robin Sharma

***

"To the victim, adversity is bad. To the leader and warrior, hard times are life's richest time of growth, opportunity, and possibility. Use them to fly."

~Robin Sharma

***

"Happiness is the precursor to success, not the result of success."

~ Shawn Achor

***

"If you want something you've never had, you must be willing to do something you've never done."

~ Thomas Jefferson

***

"Your idea of success needn't look like anyone else's."

~ Unknown

Wisdom

"Logic will take you from A-Z, but imagination will take you everywhere."

~ Albert Einstein

***

"Everybody is a genius. But if you judge a fish by its ability to climb a tree, it will live its whole life believing that it is stupid."

~ Albert Einstein

"It is the mark of an educated mind to be able to entertain a thought without accepting it."

~ Aristotle

***

"Keep away from people who try to belittle your ambitions. Small people always do that, but the really great make you feel that you too can become great."

~ Mark Twain

***

"You cannot change your destination overnight, but you can change your direction overnight."

~ Jim Rohn

***

"The most valuable thing you can make is a mistake —you can't learn anything from being perfect."

~ Adam Osborne

"Genius is seeing what everyone else sees and
thinking what no one else has thought."
~ *Albert Szent-Györgyi de Nagyrápolt*

***

"A wise man learns from his mistakes, but the wisest
of men will learn from other people's mistakes."
~ *Unknown*

***

"Remember that not getting what you want is
sometimes a wonderful stroke of luck."
~ *Dalai Lama*

***

"If you want your children to be intelligent, read
them fairy tales. If you want them to be more
intelligent, read them more fairy tales."
~ *Albert Einstein*

"Not everything that counts can be measured. Not everything that can be measured counts."
~ *Albert Einstein*

***

"Not everything that is faced can be changed, but nothing can be changed until it is faced."
~ *James Baldwin*

***

"It's not uncommon for people to spend their whole lives waiting to start living."
~ *Eckhart Tolle*

***

"If a teacher is indeed wise, he does not bid you enter the house of his wisdom, but rather leads you to the threshold of your own mind."
~ *Kahlil Gibran*

"Keep me away from the wisdom which does not cry, the philosophy which does not laugh and the greatness which does not bow before children."

~ Kahlil Gibran

***

"Say not, I have found 'the' truth, but rather, I have found 'a' truth."

~ Kahlil Gibran

***

"Life is like riding a bicycle. To keep your balance, you must keep moving."

~ Albert Einstein

***

"Identify your problems but give your power and energy to solutions."

~ Tony Robbins

"We cannot solve our problems with the same thinking we used to create them."
~ *Albert Einstein*

***

"Luck is what happens when preparation meets opportunity."
~ *Walt Disney*

***

"You cannot change the people around you, but you can change the people you choose to be around."
~ *Unknown*

***

"I have learned silence from the talkative, toleration from the intolerant, and kindness from the unkind."
~ *Kahlil Gibran*

"Be careful when following the herd. You might step in poop."

~ Unknown

***

"A lie can travel half way around the world while the truth is putting on its shoes."

~ Mark Twain

***

"If you don't know what you're looking for, how will you know it when you find it?"

~ Unknown

***

"The future depends on what we do in the present."

~ Mahatma Gandhi

"All life is an experiment. The more experiments you make the better."

~ Ralph Waldo Emerson

***

"Meditation brings wisdom. Lack of meditation leaves ignorance. Know well what leads you forward and what holds you back, and choose the path that leads to wisdom."

~ Buddha

***

"The secret of health for both mind and body is not to mourn for the past, worry about the future, or anticipate troubles, but to live in the present moment wisely and earnestly."

~ Buddha

"Insanity is doing the same thing over and over again and expecting different results."
~ *Albert Einstein*

***

"Ego has a voracious appetite. The more you feed it, the hungrier it gets."
~ *Nathaniel Bronner Jr.*

***

"Our cages are often illusory. And the key we seek is in our own pocket."
~ *Anam Cara Cat*

***

"Believe nothing, no matter where you read it, or who has said it, no matter if I have said it, unless it agrees with your own reason and your own common sense."
~ *Buddha*

"If you have fear of some pain or suffering, you should examine whether there is anything you can do about it. If you can, there is no need to worry about it. If you cannot do anything, then there is also no need to worry."

~ Dalai Lama

***

"It's better to travel well than to arrive."

~ Buddha

***

"Give me six hours to cut down a tree and I will spend the first four sharpening the axe."

~ Abraham Lincoln

***

"Sometimes you put walls up not to keep people out, but to see who cares enough to break them down."

~ Socrates

"The key is to keep company with people who uplift you, whose presence calls forth your best."

~ Epictetus

***

"Don't let your happiness depend on something you may lose."

~ C.S. Lewis

***

"Give someone a fish and you feed him for a day. Teach someone to fish and you feed him for a lifetime."

~ Lao Tzu

***

"It's none of your business what people think of you, and vice versa."

~ Unknown

"It's better to be prepared for an opportunity and not have one than to have an opportunity and not be prepared."
~ *Mark Victor Hansen*

***

"You can't start the next chapter of your life if you keep re-reading the last one."
~ *Michael McMillan*

***

"Don't put the key to your happiness in someone else's pocket."
~ *Unknown*

***

"Be grateful when you don't know something for it gives you the opportunity to learn."
~ *Unknown*

"Surrender isn't synonymous with stagnation. Sometimes accepting what is releases resistance and opens up the possibility for what could be."

~ Anam Cara Cat

***

"Knowing exactly where you want to go makes it so much easier to get there."

~ Anam Cara Cat

***

"If you let your happiness lie in the hands of another, it will always be out of reach."

~ Anam Cara Cat

***

"Every adversity brings with it the seed of an equivalent advantage."

~ Napoleon Hill

"Lessons are often repeated until they are learned."

~ Unknown

***

"A second chance doesn't mean anything if you haven't learned from your first mistake."

~ Unknown

***

"The man who does not read good books has no advantage over the man who cannot read them."

~ Mark Twain

***

"A drowning person cannot help someone else who is drowning."

~ Charles F. Glassman

"By three methods we may learn wisdom: first, by reflection, which is noblest; second, by imitation, which is easiest; third, by experience, which is the bitterest."

~ Confucius

***

"When you say yes to others, make sure you are not saying no to yourself."

~ Paulo Coelho

***

"We can learn from a teacher, but in order to become a master, we must become the teacher."

~ Charles F. Glassman

***

"Never let perfect stand in the way of good."

~ Unknown

... ♥ ...

Teaching Happiness

The best way to introduce the subject of Happiness is to begin by asking questions to prompt curiosity, critical thinking, and conversation: (Find teaching resources including complete unit and lesson plans to address the social-emotional domain on my web site: www.anamcaracat.com)

I.   Ask students what society typically teaches about the formula for success and happiness. Chances are they will relay the all too familiar equation:

hard work = success = happiness

Challenge that equation by asking what the potential hazards might be of following such a system. Then, explain that *lasting* happiness is a *precursor* to success not a *result* of success, and have them consider the benefits of the following formula:

happiness = passionate pursuits = success

II. Have students watch and discuss Shawn Achor's Ted Talk *Happy Secret to Better Work* available on the GoodThink web site: www.goodthinkinc.com/resources/videos

III. Ask students to brainstorm characteristics happy people possess that undoubtedly contribute to success.

Psychologists and neuroscientists know that happy people are:

- more intelligent
- more intuitive
- more productive
- more efficient
- better at problem-solving /critical thinking
- more optimistic
- more energetic
- more creative
- more resilient
- more adaptable to change
- have more self-confidence/self-esteem
- more pleasant to be around
- have stronger interpersonal and intrapersonal skills

IV. Ask students to research the four major chemicals that contribute to the feeling of happiness and affect learning, memory, cognition, and emotion:

- **Dopamine**: Dopamine is the feel-good neurotransmitter that's released in the brain when we're rewarded for something or anticipating a pleasurable event. It affects memory, attention, and cognition.

- **Serotonin**: Serotonin is a neurotransmitter that is believed to affect mood, anxiety, and happiness levels. 80-90% of serotonin lives in the gut, so these levels are largely influenced by food we eat, particularly foods containing tryptophan, tyrosine, and micronutrients.

- **Oxytocin:** Oxytocin, commonly known as the brain's "love drug," is a hormone that acts as a neurotransmitter which is released through physical as well as social bonding when we feel cared for, safe, and secure.

- **Endorphins:** Endorphins are opioid neuropeptides that produce a morphine-like chemical that is often released through physical activity and can create a sense of euphoria and reduce stress and pain.

V.   Ask students if they think the brain is fixed or if it's possible to change or rewire it.

Have them research neuroplasticity and "fixed mindset vs growth mindset."

- Scientists now know the brain, though once believed to be fixed, is actually able to restructure itself by creating new neural networks. This allows self-defeating patterns of belief and behavior to be replaced with positive, proactive practices that can transform one's perspective and quality of life.

VI.   Ask students if they'd be willing to "test" the idea that increased happiness leads to increased success with a 21 day trial study. Begin by having them document their present levels of happiness on a scale of 1-10 prior to starting the experiment. Ask them to identify the areas of their lives that would likely improve if they felt happier, and have them create a few short-term goals. Then, challenge them to manage and maintain their emotional health by committing to at least 3-5 of the daily activities known to restructure the chemical makeup of the brain. Every practice listed below has been clinically proven to increase the production of dopamine, serotonin, oxytocin, endorphins, or a combination thereof. Keep in mind that some of these activities, such as daily gratitude journaling and reading and reflecting on inspirational quotes (Birdseed), can be easily integrated into daily classroom routines:

- Exercising
- Daily gratitude journaling
- Participating in social activities or community groups such as sports, yoga, youth groups,

church, Boy/Girl Scouts, art classes, dance classes, writing groups, or hiking groups

- Meditating
- Reading and reflecting on inspirational texts and quotes
- Reflecting daily on core values and principles
- Helping others by way of intentional acts of kindness
- Getting plenty of sunshine
- Listening to positive, uplifting music
- Positive self-talk or affirmations
- Deciding on a "Life Purpose" and learning something new every day related to that purpose
- Practicing creative visualization, wherein you imagine yourself living out your ideal scenarios (create a vision board)
- Practicing compassion and showing empathy towards all people (even those you don't particularly like or understand)
- Volunteering at a local charity, library, or animal sanctuary or shelter
- Singing
- Laughing
- Learning to play an instrument

- Giving/receiving long hugs
- Cuddling/playing with animals
- Creating daily to-do lists with goals that can easily be checked off (as opposed to *only* having big long-term goals for the future)
- Eating foods rich in tryptophan, tyrosine (amino acids), and polyphenols (micronutrients) that boost dopamine and serotonin production in the brain such as almonds, kiwi, bananas, kale, apples, green tea, strawberries and blueberries, dark chocolate, & beets

Have students create a chart wherein they list their chosen activities to check off daily as completed. Be sure to emphasize that it takes time for new neuropathways and new habits to become ingrained in the brain. Until these activities are practiced daily for *at least* 21 consecutive days, the commitment might feel like a strained effort—but after 21 days, their practices will feel like a natural part of their daily routines, which means feeling happy every day will be an automatic habit.

It's important to mention that it's crucial for you, as the teacher, to consciously model this proactive behavior and exemplify sound emotional intelligence. Kids can't be what they don't see, and if you don't authentically embody the principles you're teaching, it's less likely you will influence students' paradigms, much less their behaviors. If your students commit to using a daily chart or checklist to remind them of the suggested "mood-boosting" activities, consider doing it along with them. Create and display your own Mood Booster Board and decide on the 5 most important practices you will commit to for the next 21 days inside and outside of school. As they see you checking off the boxes daily, the importance of the positive behaviors will be reinforced, and, in addition to inspiring them, after the 21 days, you can speak with authority on the effects of activities.

VII.   Formally follow up with students after they complete the 21 day challenge. Allow them to discuss their findings as a group and then have them write a reflection on their personal experiences. Ask students to specifically note their pre and post-trial levels of happiness, the degree to which they maintained their daily mood-boosting activities, and the extent to which enhanced levels of positivity helped them achieve their goals. Be sure to share your own findings as well.

Suggested Resources

Anam Cara Cat's Complete Units and Lesson Plans to Foster Emotional Intelligence: **www.anamcaracat.com** *or* **https://www.teacherspayteachers.com/Store/Anam-Cara-Cat**

Emotional Intelligence: Why it Can Matter More Than IQ by Daniel Goleman

The Happiness Advantage by Shawn Achor

The How of Happiness: A Scientific Approach to Getting the Life You Want by Sonja Lyubomirsky

The Emotional Life of Your Brain: How Its Unique Patterns Affect the Way You Think, Feel and Live—And How You Can Change Them by Richard J. Davidson

Shawn Achor Co-Founder and CEO of GoodThink
www.goodthinkinc.com

Charles F. Glassman, MD, FACP
www.charlesglassmanmd.com

Contributors:

Abraham Lincoln: 16th President of the United States; led US through civil war and abolished slavery (1809–1865)

Adam Osborne: British author and computer designer (1939–2003)

Aesop: Greek storyteller (620–564 BCE)

Albert Einstein: German physicist who developed the theory of relativity; awarded the Nobel Prize in physics (1879–1955)

Albert Schweitzer: German theologian, physician, and Nobel Peace Prize recipient (1875–1965)

Albert Szent-Gyorgyi: Hungarian physiologist who discovered vitamin C (1893–1986)

Alexander Graham Bell: Scottish scientist, inventor, and engineer credited with invented the first telephone (1847–1922)

Anam Cara Cat: Catrina Lee - American inspirational author, teacher, and artist of life.
http://www.anamcaracat.com/

Anais Nin: Cuban-American author (1903–1977)

Anatole France: French poet and journalist (1844–1924)

Andre Gide: French author and recipient of Nobel Peace Prize in Literature (1869–1951)

Anne Frank: Jewish Holocaust victim and writer (1929–1945)

Anne Lamott: American writer, speaker, and political activist

Aristotle: Greek philosopher and scientist (384–322 BC)

Arnold Palmer: American professional golfer

Ashley Hodgeson: American writer

Benjamin Disraeli: British politician and writer (1804–1881)

Bernard Meltzer: American radio show host (1916–1998)

Bob Dylan: American singer-songwriter

Booker T. Washington: African-American civil rights activist, educator, author (1856–1915)

Brian Littrell: American singer-songwriter

Brian Tracey: Canadian author, entrepreneur, and personal development leader

Buddha: Indian prince, believed to have renounced worldly pleasures in search of enlightenment; also known as Siddhartha Gautama; teachings are the foundation of Buddhism. (563 BCE–483 BCE)

Buckminster Fuller: American architect, author, designer, inventor (1895–1983)

Byron Katie: American speaker and author

Carl Jung: Swiss psychiatrist and founder of analytical psychology (1875–1961)

Charles F. Glassman: American MD and wellness coach.

Charles Swindoll: American author, educator, and preacher

Chip Conley: American author and hospitality expert

Christine Arlo: American author and inspirational speaker

Ester Hicks: American inspirational author and speaker

Florence Scovel Shin: American artist and illustrator (1871–1940)

Frank A. Clark: American screenwriter (1888–1962)

Frank Zappa: American musician and songwriter (1940–1993)

G.B. Stern: English novelist (1890–1973)

George Bernard Shaw: Irish playwright and political activist (1856–1950)

George Elliot: Pen name for English writer, Mary Ann Evans (1819–1880)

Grayson Marshall: American motivational speaker and former athlete

Harriet Tubman: African-American abolitionist and humanitarian (1822–1913)

Helen Keller: American author, speaker, and political activist; first deafblind person to earn a Bachelor's degree (1880–1968)

Henry David Thoreau: American writer, philosopher, abolitionist, (1817–1862)

Henry Emerson Fosdick: American pastor (1878–1969)

Henry Ford: American industrialist and founder of Ford Motor Company (1863–1947)

Herman Melville: American novelist; author *Moby Dick* (1819–1891)

H. Jackson Brown: American author

Horace Flaccus: Roman Poet (65–8 BC)

Howard Thurman: African-American author, civil rights leader, educator, philosopher, and theologian (1899–1981)

James Allen: English writer (1864–1912)

James Baldwin: American playwright, poet, social critic, and novelist (1924–1987)

Jimmy Dean: American singer, actor, and business man (1928–2010)

Jim Rohn: American entrepreneur, author, motivational speaker (1930–2009)

JK Rowling: British novelist; best known for *Harry Potter* novels

Johann Wolfgang Von Goethe: German writer and politician (1749–1832)

John Adams: 2nd President of the United States and 1st vice president (1735–1826)

John Burroughs: American naturalist and writer (1837–1921)

John E. Southard: American technology planner and academic administrator

John Lennon: English singer-songwriter; co-founder of the Beatles rock band (1940–1980)

John Mason: American inspirational author, publisher, and speaker

John Milton: English poet (1608–1674)

John Rockefeller: American founder of oil company, businessman, philanthropist (1839–1937)

John Wooden: American basketball player and coach (1910–2010)

Jonatan Martensson: American inspirational author

Jonathan Lockwood Huie: American inspirational author and speaker

Joseph Wirthlin: American businessman and religious leader (1917–2008)

Joseph Campbell: American mythologist and lecturer (1904–1987)

Joyce Brothers: American psychologist and columnist (1927–2013)

J.P. Morgan: American banker and philanthropist (1837–1913)

Kahlil Gibran: Lebanese artist and poet (1883–1931)

Kak Sri: Kashmiri veterinarian and writer (1917–1993)

Kurt Vonnegut: American writer and activist

Leonardo da Vinci: Italian painter, sculptor, architect, musician, mathematician, engineer, inventor, geologist, writer, botanist, cartographer, and anatomist (1452–1519)

Lao Tzu: Chinese poet and philosopher (571 BCE–Zhou Dynasty)

Lou Holtz: American football player analyst for ESPN

Lucius Seneca: Roman philosopher (4 BC–65 AD)

Mahatma Gandhi: Mohandas Karamchand Gandhi: Indian civil rights leader; led India to independence using nonviolent civil disobedience (1869–1948)

Malala Yousafzai: Pakistani activist and youngest Nobel Prize recipient

Malcom S. Forbes: American entrepreneur and publisher of Forbes magazine (1919–1990)

Marcus Aurelius: Roman emperor (121–180 AD)

Maria Robinson: First female president of Ireland

Mark Victor Hansen: American inspirational author and motivational speaker. Co-creator for *Chicken Soup for the Soul* series

Mark Twain: American author and humorist; best known for Tom Sawyer and Huckleberry Finn novels (1835–1910)

Margaret Mead: American cultural anthropologist (1901–1978)

Marianne Williamson: American author, speaker, and spiritual leader

Marilyn vos Savant: American columnist and playwright known for having highest IQ in Guinness Book of Records

Martin Luther King Jr: African-American civil rights leader, activist, humanitarian (1929–1968)

Marvin Williams: African-American pastor and author

Mary Anne Radmacher: American writer and artist

Mary Engelbreit: American graphic artist and children's book illustrator

Maya Angelou: American author, poet, dancer, actor, singer (1928–2014)

Michael Jordan: American professional basketball player

Michael McMillian: American writer and actor

Michelangelo di Lodovico Buonarroti Simoni: Italian sculptor, painter, architect, poet and engineer (1475–1564)

Milton Berle: American comedian and actor (1908–2002)

Mother Teresa: Roman Catholic missionary (1910–1997)

Nelson Mandela: South-African anti-apartheid revolutionary, philanthropist, and president of South Africa (1918–2013)

Napoleon Bonaparte: French military and political leader (1769–1821)

Napoleon Hill: American author of Think and Grow Rich and revered success lecturer (1883–1970)

Nathaniel Bronner Jr.: American scientist and entrepreneur

Nora Roberts: American romance author

Orison Swett Marden: American inspirational author (1848–1924)

Paul Boese: American author (1923–1976)

Paulo Coelho: Brazilian writer; best known for novel *The Alchemist*

Peace Pilgrim: American spiritual teacher and activist (1908–1981)

Peter Drucker: Austrian educator and author (1909–2005)

Ralph Waldo Emerson: American essayist and poet who led the Transcendentalist movement (1803–1882)

Richard Bach: American writer

Richard L. Evans: American writer (1906–1971)

R.H. Blyth: English author (1898–1964)

Roald Dahl: British novelist, poet, screenwriter (1916–1990)

Robert Brault: American writer

Robert Frost: American Pulitzer Prize winning poet (1874–1963)

Robert Louis Stevenson: Scottish novelist, poet, and travel writer (1850–1894)

Robert Siltanen: American writer for Forbes Magazine and Apple campaign

Robin Sharma: Canadian writer and leadership expert

R. Updegraff: American author (1189–1977)

Sally Koch: American author

Samuel Johnson: English writer and lexicographer (1709–1784)

Scott Avett: American singer and songwriter

Shawn Achor: American author and positive psychology expert

Shirley MacLaine: American actress and author

Shri Kak: Kashmiri veterinarian and writer (1917–1993)

Socrates: Greek philosopher and teacher (470–399 BC)

Sonia Friedman: British Broadway theatre producer

Theodore Roosevelt: American author and 26th President of the United States (1858–1919)

Thomas Edison: American inventor and businessman (1847–1931)

Thomas Jefferson: American founding father and author of Declaration of Independence (1743–1826)

Thomas J. Watson: American businessman; CEO of IBM; (1874–1956)

Tom Krause: Finnish psychiatrist and musician (1934–2013)

Tony Robbins: American motivational speaker, life coach, self-help author

T.S. Elliot: American poet and playwright (1888–1965)

Vince Lombardi: American football player and (1913-–1970)

Virgil: Roman Poet (70 BC–19 BC)

Vista M. Kelly: American writer (1901–1988)

Vivian Greene: South-African writer (1904–2003)

Wale Ayeni: American writer

Walt Disney: cartoonist, film producer, animator, co-founder Walt Disney Company

Wayne Dyer: American writer and motivational speaker

Wayne Gretzky: Canadian hockey player

Washington Irving: American author and historian; best known for *The Legend of Sleepy Hollow* (1783–1859)

William Arthur Ward: American author (1921–1994)

William Prescott: American colonel in Revolutionary War (1726–1795)

William Shakespeare: English poet, playwright, and actor (1564–1616)

Will Smith: American actor, producer, and songwriter

W.M. Lewis: American teacher and politician (1878–1945)

W.T. Purkiser: American preacher and author (1910–1992)

Phillip Yancey: American Christian author

Yousuf Karsh: American-Canadian portrait photographer (1908–2002)

Ziad K. Abdelnour: Lebanese-American banker and activist

Zig Ziglar: American author and motivational speaker (1926–1995

About Your Author, Anam Cara Cat

"Anam cara" is an ancient Celtic term that means soul-friend.

Cat, formally known as Catrina Lee, is a secondary Special Education and Language Arts teacher who lives in Boulder, Colorado. In addition to creating innovative teaching tools, she writes inspirational fiction for children and personal development material for adults.

As the mother of two amazing humans, and a passionate animal advocate, she devotes her creative energy to inspiring and empowering others to create a more peaceful world that embraces inclusive compassion for all beings.

For more inspiration including engaging unit and lesson plans to foster the social-emotional domain, visit Cat's web site: www.anamcaracat.com

Stay connected

Web site: **www.anamcaracat.com**
where you'll find more teaching resources including
detailed unit and lesson plans to address the social-
emotional domain

Facebook: Soul Seeds & Teacher Resources by your
Anam Cara Cat

Twitter: @anamcaracat

Instagram: @anamcaracat

Pinterest: Anam Cara Cat

Gmail: **anamcaracat@gmail.com**

Teachers Pay Teachers: Anam Cara Cat
https://www.teacherspayteachers.com/Store
/Anam-Cara-Cat

Made in the USA
Monee, IL
26 August 2021

76613921R00100